10.95

D0251908

Liz Allen

improvising
better

A Guide for

the Working

Improviser

HEINEMANN
Portsmouth, NH

Heinemann
A division of Reed Elsevier Inc.
361 Hanover Street
Portsmouth, NH 03801–3912
www.heinemanndrama.com

Offices and agents throughout the world

Library of Congress Cataloging-in-Publication Data
Carrane, Jimmy.
    Improvising better : a guide for the working improviser /
Jimmy Carrane and Liz Allen.
        p. cm.
    ISBN-13: 978-0-325-00942-1
    ISBN-10: 0-325-00942-2 (pbk. : alk. paper)
    1. Improvisation (Acting). I. Allen, Liz (Elizabeth). II. Title.

PN2071.I5C24 2006
792.02′8—dc22   2006014781

Acquisitions editor: Lisa A. Barnett
Production: Lynne Costa
Cover design: Night & Day Design
Typesetter: Tom Allen/Pear Graphic Design
Manufacturing: Steve Bernier

Printed in the United States of America on acid-free paper
10 09 08 07 06   VP   1 2 3 4 5

Contents

Acknowledgments

*T*his has been the hardest part for us to write, the acknowledgments, the thank-yous, to the people who made this book possible. We hope that we haven't forgotten someone. If we have, we apologize, and we'll try to include you in the film version.

First we'd like thank the many students who have studied with us in our classes and our workshops over the years. Thank you for helping us with our research. We'd like to thank the many teams we were lucky to be a part of as performers or directors—Jazz Freddy, Frank Booth, Valhalla, The Neighbors, My Naked Friends, Mission Improvable, The Comedy Underground, Tequila Mockingbird, The Armando Diaz Experience, =e, Deep Schwa, The IO Roadshow, Summer Rental, Veto Power, Fatty Four Eyes, Gambrinus King of Beer, WakaMalaka, and Naked, because without them we would have just written about ourselves.

We would like to thank all the wonderful teachers who have influenced us over the years and dedicated their lives to this art form: Dan Bakedahl, Matt Besser, Jack Bronis, Craig Cackowski, Jim Carlson, Matt Chapman, Stephen Colbert, Bob Dassie, Jim Dennen, Armando Diaz, Kevin Dorff, Rachel Dratch, Molly Erdman, Tina Fey, Neil Flynn, Lillie Frances, Michael Gellman, Megan Grano, Noah Gregoropoulous, Paul Grondy, Peter Gwinn, John Herizol, Norm Holly, Steven Ivcich, TJ Jagadowski, Nick Johne, Matt Kaye, David Koechner, Anne Libera, John Lutz, Mary McCain, Rob Mello, Susan Messing, Greg Mills, Kevin Mullaney, Colleen Murray, Mike Myers, Tim O'Malley, Dave Pasquesi, Jonathan Pitts, Brian Posen, Rich Prouty, Dave Razowski, Gary Rudoren, Sue Salvi, Al Samuels, Abby Sher, Miles Stroth, Rich Talarico, Craig Uhlir, Jean Villepique, and Matt Walsh.

And especially thanks to Del Close and Martin de Maat, two of the most powerful teachers in this art form. Although they definitely worked different sides of the improv street, they often got the same results. We are forever grateful for their contributions.

We would like to thank our pseudo literary agent Josh Karp, our business advisor Todd Logan, and our legal counsel Doug Edwards, for without them we would have gone crazy. Thanks to our "editorial" board Bob Dassie, Homer Marrs, Amanda Blake Davis, Jeff Griggs, and Stephnie Weir, who gave us great feedback and caught most of our typos. Thanks to Kelly Leonard at The Second City for his constant support . . . by the way, we're available for a touring company when there's an opening. . . . And thanks also to Mick Napier and Jennifer Estlin at the Annoyance Theater in Chicago, who answered a million questions, and hooked us up with the wonderful Lisa Barnett at Heinemann Publishing. A big thanks to Lynne Costa at Heinemann for taking us down the home stretch.

A big thanks goes to Charna Halpern, "The First Lady of Improv" at the iOChicago Theater (always the Improv Olympic to us), where we learned the most as performers and teachers, and sometimes even as people. And our final thanks goes to the city of Chicago, for lending our book some of its spirit and character; still the best place to study improv.

Preface
Why We Wrote Our Book

We were both teaching improv in Chicago in 2003 when one of us placed a phone call to the other about some improv-related advice. (Liz claims Jimmy called to baby-sit. Jimmy claims he called for a specific teaching exercise. At the printing of this book, the matter remains unresolved.)

That conversation turned into a workshop. That workshop turned into many workshops. The next thing we knew people from all over the city and then throughout the country came to Chicago to take our workshop. We were overwhelmed by the response.

What we didn't know was that while we were teaching these workshops, we were collecting data from our students. It didn't matter what part of the country the students were from, we started to see that improvisers everywhere were struggling with the same issues.

So, we decided to share this data with improvisers in Chicago in a little marketing piece entitled "Top Ten Blind Spots for Improvisers." These were ten specific patterns we saw in improvisers that we felt were holding them back from becoming the great improvisers they were capable of being. We thought this was important information to share, and evidently others did, too.

We got some great feedback from the "Top Ten Blind Spots for Improvisers." Some of that feedback was that we should write a book. So here is that book.

How to Read Our Book | *1*

*I*n writing this book we wanted to give you, as closely as possible, the experience of taking our workshop. Which, in hindsight, we realize was pretty difficult. We'd like to think that in our workshops we break people down a bit, and then build them back up. So in this chapter, we're attempting to do that, break you down and build you up. We just wish we had six hours to hammer home the two following points like we do in the workshops.

So keep the following two points in mind as you read our book.

Point 1: You Bought This Book, So You Must Have Talent

One of the most frequently asked questions we get from our students, and frankly one we can't stand, is, "Do I have what it takes to do this?" We are polite to them. But really, they are wasting our time, because we don't have the answer. It's not our call, and it never has been. It's their call. We are teachers, not psychics.

Here's what we do know. If you want to improvise, we want to help you. We are already impressed because you bought our book, which means on some level you want to get better. That's enough for us, and it should be enough for you. Not only are we grateful that you bought our book and that you're recommending it to all your friends, we are also glad to see you're willing to push yourself to the next level of your development.

If you have a desire to do this work and you're already in class or doing a show, you're doing the work; you're improvising. You are in. No one can vote you off this island, except you and your low self-esteem. So, shut up, stop whining, and improvise. We are not going to have this discussion again.

Point 2: There's Only One Way to Improvise

Yours. Our job as teachers, and in this case, writers, is to help you find your voice. Improv is a very personal art form. It has never been a one-size-fits-all kind of thing. So, what works for one person may not work for another. And thank God for that. We hope you get a lot out of this book, but we are realistic—we know that not every chapter will apply to you specifically and that's fine. These aren't the last words on improv. These aren't the first words on improv. These are just our words on improv.

Although we promote specific concepts of improvisation that have worked for us over many years of performing, directing and teaching, we by no means are saying there is a right and wrong way to improvise. That would be danger-ous. In writing this book, just like when we are teaching our workshops, we can only share with you our experiences. That is what good teachers do.

And there are a lot of good teachers out there, besides Jimmy and besides Liz. The more experiences from teach-ers you have, the more you'll have to draw from and the more tools you'll have in your improv tool box. We didn't learn from one person, we learned from many. So just like an improviser, every teacher comes from his or her own perspective. Find those teachers. That is your job, that is your journey as an improviser.

There is a saying, but we don't know to whom to attribute it: Take what works and leave the rest. Please keep that saying in mind while reading this book.

What Happened to Yes? 2

Yes the yesser.
— PAUL GRONDY

One of the most surprising things we've noticed in our workshops is the general lack of agreement. It is the heart of this work, duh, but agreement skills tend to drop as other techniques are learned. It seems people want to create something quick and manufactured instead of simply saying *yes* to others' ideas.

These improvisers hold back, waiting for an idea to spark them. They cherry-pick, becoming selective on what to say *yes* to, thinking they can predict which idea will be the most successful. But if they said *yes* to every idea, every idea would be successful.

Something weird seems to happen after people get about a year and a half of improvising under their belts. They think they're cleverer than *yes*. All of a sudden, they think they are so sophisticated that they are above saying *yes*. Saying *yes* becomes too remedial.

The irony is that the most sophisticated players always return to old-fashioned *yes*. A high-level player craves saying *yes*, and looks forward to the challenge of making all ideas, especially the implausible ones, work. That is truly improvising. The beauty of this work is the element of surprise to your partner, to the audience, and to yourself. And the best way to assure surprise is good old-fashioned agreement, made by scratch, not some store-bought brand.

A Few Solutions . . .

EXERCISE 1: OVERLAPPING YES

This exercise is a high-energy reminder of the fun, excitement, and pure entertainment of *yes*, even if you're saying *yes* to nothing. *Yes* is an energy. It's a vibration. It's something you can feel in your bones. In this exercise, *yes* can be accomplished without content.

How It Works

Two people sit face to face in chairs. One of them begins speaking, just as himself, not in a scene. Such as, "I really like your shirt." The other person immediately begins nodding his head up and down, already agreeing with his body, and says, "Yes! Yes! I like my shirt, too!" before the first person's sentence is even completed. This is overlapping *yes*. This is the only exercise you'll read in this book that condones interrupting one another, so enjoy it.

PERSON #1: I like my shirt! It's got stripes . . .
PERSON #2: Yes, stripes, stripes! Yes, they're like a tiger . . .
PERSON #1: Yes! Tigers are the best! Yes! I love the zoo!
PERSON #2: I love the zoo! Yes! Yes . . .
PERSON #1: When can we go to the zoo?
PERSON #2: Yes! The zoo! Yes! Let's go now!

These two people should crescendo to a frenzied peak of *yes!*, be on their feet shouting agreements at one another, overlapping their words, and tripping over each other to agree.

Variation

A good wrap-up after everyone's had a turn is a group Over-lapping Yes session. Everyone stands in a circle, they all start simultaneously, and agree as a group. This is a great energy builder.

Teaching Tip

When doing this exercise, there should not be any silence between the two people or the group at all. The overlapping begins immediately. If the players are stiff or resistant, or self-conscious, then have them drop the dialogue, and simply repeat the word *yes* until they build to a frenzied peak of *yes*. Then get them to stand up. Have them switch chairs. Do what you have to to keep them saying *yes*.

EXERCISE 2: THE SILENT SUPPORTER

This is a great exercise to show how you can agree without words.

How It Works

Three players perform a scene; one of those players will remain silent throughout the scene. The silent person will not be assigned. Instead, the three players will discover who is silent as the scene progresses. Since there are only three people in this exercise, and one is non-speaking, the group should able to determine who is silent within the first few minutes of the scene. We've found this exercise works best without taking a suggestion from the audience—the three just get onstage and go.

Once it has been determined who the silent person is, that player will need to discover ways to support the scene without words or taking focus. Here's an example:

PERSON #1: Of course Dad's not talking to you after what you said at breakfast.
PERSON #2: Yeah, you're right. Dad, I'm sorry.
PERSON #3: (the silent Dad turns away grumpily and picks up the newspaper, ignoring the apology.)

Now we have the foundation of a strong relationship

scene, and we know that throughout the scene Dad will remain silent. He could support the scene by continuing to ignore his family, or by getting up and locking himself in the basement, or by calmly working on his crossword. Dad infuriates his family with his passive aggressive behavior. Ideally, throughout the scene, the silent person and talkers will work off of each other.

Teaching Tip

It's important for the other two people to protect the silent person from looking dumb. From our example, the talkers can't demand that Dad talk, because it's established that he won't. Also, the silent person can be environment, such as a bear rug or a gondola driver or a corpse. Of course these should be chosen to help, not hinder, the scene.

Sometimes the silent improvisor panics when he realizes he has to be silent. He stops listening to the talkers. Also, the talkers stop paying attention to the silent one, thinking he's unimportant since he's not talking. If this happens, slow everyone down, and remind them to listen to each other.

Warning Label

This is not charades. This is not a guessing game or a mime exercise. Don't let the talkers try to communicate to the silent person with their hands.

Nice People + Nice Choices = Boring Scenes

3

> If you're not going to react to
> hot coffee on your crotch,
> then what are you going to react to?
> —BOB DASSIE

Not much makes us sadder than seeing technically strong, talented, and gifted improvisers onstage playing really nice characters making really nice choices. These are usually really boring scenes. Don't get us wrong. We like to work with nice people, we like to be around nice people, heck, we *are* nice people. We just don't want to see them onstage. Instead, we want to see improvisers taking care of their partners, and their characters taking care of themselves.

Nobody wants to offend, but everybody wants to do good scene work. *You can't have it both ways.* What we've seen is when students do take a risk and speak the uncomfortable stuff onstage, suddenly they realize how much more energized and alive their choices are. And they are giving something substantial to the scene at the same time. Strong, bold, honest statements (the kind that make a nice person squirm) are the best gifts of all.

This whole nicey-nice syndrome results in boring scenes. Stop being so damn nice and play life! We want to see two selfish characters fighting for what they want. Give yourself permission to emotionally hurt your partner's character onstage, and they should do the same to you. So, take the plastic wrap off your improv and let your characters get down and dirty.

A Few Solutions . . .

EXERCISE 1: THE VULNERABLE CIRCLE

This exercise is the first step in getting an improviser to replace the instinct of being nice with the instinct of being vulnerable.

How It Works

The entire group stands in a circle with one person in the middle of the circle. We'll call this middle person Joe. Joe turns to each person in the surrounding circle and tells each person something personal about himself; something he wouldn't normally share with a stranger at a cocktail party. He will say something that is intimate and personal, as if he is talking to a close friend, such as, "I haven't talked my parents in years," or " I am afraid of commitment," or "I feel like everyone is better than I am."

The idea is for Joe to be vulnerable and begin sharing as himself. This causes a deeper and more sincere connection with the entire ensemble and will make it easier for Joe's characters to be more vulnerable in his scene work. When Joe has gone around the circle and interacted with each person once, his turn is complete. He will be replaced by someone else in the circle until the entire group has had a turn sharing of themselves.

Remember, being *vulnerable* diverts being *nice*. Sharing something about yourself can be difficult for you or the person hearing the news, and it might spark emotional responses in a scene, and this is a good thing! You are connecting. People hide behind *nice* because they are afraid of not being liked. The Vulnerable Circle encourages sharing feelings and interrupts the instinct to be nice.

Teaching Tips

While teaching this exercise, sometimes we have experienced that people freeze up and become stuck. Sharing something intimate about yourself, especially to a group of people, can be difficult.

As the teacher/director, feel free to prompt the middle person (Joe) with specific questions. We recommend you create a list of twelve to fifteen questions and bring them into your class/rehearsal so you don't get stuck, too. We have found this frees the improvisers from overthinking and putting too much pressure on themselves.

Questions we have used:

> When was the last time you cried?
> What is your biggest fear onstage?
> What is one thing you hate about your parents?
> What is one thing you love about your parents?
> The body part you love?
> The body part you hate?
> What makes you mad?
> You are a good friend because you are_____.
> What is one thing you would change about your personality?
> What is your biggest regret?
> What is your biggest goal for yourself?

Eventually, the goal is to encourage each person to share without the prompting questions. Then they have reached a trust level with the group that will help eliminate niceness.

And remind everyone: what is shared within the group, stays within the group.

Warning Label

This is not therapy. It's important that at the beginning of this exercise the director/teacher stresses that this is not therapy and that the issues revealed are resolved within the revealer. We recommend you start the exercise by saying to everyone, "Please only reveal what you're comfortable with. Think of something specific about yourself that the group probably does not know about you, but make sure you are resolved about what you share."

EXERCISE 2: ROUND ROBIN OF "BLURT"

The purpose of this exercise is to get the improviser to feel his very first instincts and to make a statement based on the connection between him and his partner.

How It Works

One person (let's use Joe again) stands with the entire team in a line facing him. Each person in the line will take a turn and stand in front of Joe. They will connect momentarily by standing face to face and making eye contact. Then Joe will blurt something out, a statement based on the connection he feels from his partner. It can be raw, like, "You have great tits," or, "You are a weasel and I'll never forgive you for what you did." Or it can be something more scenic, like, "This is the last funeral I'll go to for anyone in your family. Too many people die in your family. I'm done."

Then the other person will blurt something back. Their response should be almost an emotional, knee-jerk response to the statement. (Agreement is always good, too.) For instance, Joe's partner could respond to the last statement above in various ways: "For God's sake, it's not my fault my family keeps dying. Good, then, I don't have to be embarrassed by how drunk you get at funerals." Or, "Fine, then I'm not going either, and I'll use you as my excuse."

Then that person goes to the back of the line and Joe is joined by the next person in line and repeats the blurt process again, making a whole new statement from the connection. When we go once through the line with Joe, we get someone else to take Joe's place, until the entire group each gets a turn.

Teaching Tips

The most important aspect of this exercise is for the improviser to work organically off his partner. The "blurts" really must come from the connection between each person. What you hope to accomplish with this exercise is to have each improviser override his brain and work from feelings, since feelings are the basis of the connection between two people. Just feel it and say it, especially if it isn't nice. Just blurt it out.

One way to make sure the "blurts" come off their partners and are in-the-moment is to coach the improvisers to *slow down*. If the teacher/director feels that they are not getting the "blurt" from their partner but instead have pre-planned their responses, feel free to restart the pair by giving them a couple of seconds in silence. Have them look into each other's eyes and take some time to reconnect.

Then the teacher/director can ask pointed questions about the relationship of the two players. If you notice the pair may be attracted to each other, ask one of them if that is true. If she says yes, then have her speak to it. If she says, "You have a nice mouth," encourage her to go deeper, by asking her, what do you really mean? If she ends up saying to her partner, "I'd like to have sex with you on the floor right now," you know they have made intimate and personal connection because that's raw and real.

Note: Depending on the level of improviser, you may want to just have them make that primal connection and then do a second round with them making statements, and again, feel free to coach them through all rounds. Take the example we just used: "I want to have sex with you on the floor." Now have them turn that into a scenic statement, such as: "Kelly, my parents won't be home for another couple hours and my brother gave me a condom." What a fun line to respond to.

Now, not all improvisers work at the same speed. Believe it or not, some improvisers benefit from going faster, especially if they are connecting with their partners, but seem to be editing their "blurts." Speed the exercise up on them.

Ideally everyone will connect with their partners immediately and blurt things out unedited, whipping right through this exercise.

Warning Label

This exercise requires you to use your teaching instincts, and if you as teacher/director have not worked this way, have patience with yourself! Learning to perceive how connected players are to each other is a skill you will develop over time. Also, use the class if you are stuck. Ask the ensemble, "What are you picking up from them?" This keeps them involved and sometimes they will surprise you with their keen insights.

Anger Is Okay | 4

Never apologize for showing your feelings.
When you do, you apologize for the truth.
—BENJAMIN DISRAELI

O ne of the strongest trends we've noticed is the lack of anger in scenes. This really frustrates us. We feel improvisers confuse anger and agreement, thinking the two can't exist at the same time.

Look, there's no doubt that there is a rule of improv: avoid conflict. But this rule doesn't mean avoid anger. It means avoid reacting to conflicts with disagreement. See, it boils down to *conflicts with anger and disagreement* versus *conflicts with anger and agreement*. The latter is fine. Anger is an emotion. Anger is a great catalyst for transformation.

Here's an example of a conflict with anger and disagreement:

> HUSBAND (to wife): You're having an affair.
> WIFE (angrily): You bastard, you're never going to trust me, are you?
> HUSBAND: I saw the way you looked at him.
> WIFE: I liked his suit!

The opening statement is a great beginning to a scene, but when it incites anger with disagreement, the scene gets stuck. The two characters are just blaming one another, stuck in denial, and can't transform.

Instead, here's an example of a conflict with anger and agreement:

> HUSBAND (to wife): You're having an affair.
>
> WIFE (relieved): Yes, I am. There! I said it. Gosh, I feel better.
>
> HUSBAND (getting angry): You promised the landscaper would be the last one.
>
> WIFE: I know, I'm sorry. I'm not very good at keeping promises.

There we have an obvious conflict, an affair, and a character justifiably angry, but they are not stuck. That scene clearly can transform.

If you refuse to get angry, you are refusing transformation. So give your character permission to get angry, really angry. But remember: *Don't get stuck in anger!* If argument comes up, agree through it. If your character gets so angry he or she wants to stage hit your scene partner, do it (using stage combat, of course). The more committed you are to it, the faster it will transform to the next emotion.

Take, for example, an argument from your real life. One minute you can be raving mad at someone, then laughing, then sad, then disgusted, and then all the way back to raving mad. You organically moved through these emotions. See, once you exhaust one emotion, you automatically move to the next one. That is transformation.

The other thing players seem to miss about anger is: it is a gift. When a character in a scene genuinely gets angry, we get to see that character express anger, then another character responds to that anger, and surprising discoveries are almost guaranteed. And this is a good thing for a scene. It's a gift. A genuine gift, remember, is when you give your partner something strong to react to. That's a gift. Got it? Let's move on, we're getting pissed.

A VERY SPECIAL WARNING LABEL

With higher level improvisers, we've seen that the opposite is true: These people use anger as a crutch. Anger becomes the go-to emotion. We really think it's a fear of being vulnerable. These people don't let anger transform, they get stuck in it.

One trick we have found that is helpful in breaking this pattern is to have the character replace his typically angry response with a vulnerable admission.

For example, here's an angry scene:

PERSON #1: Hey, Fred, I noticed you punched in late this morning.

FRED: Hey, what's it to you? I'm the boss, you don't tell me what to do.

PERSON #1: I was just trying to see if everything's okay with you.

FRED: Stay out of my business.

This scene will lead nowhere but an argument if these two aren't careful. Let's try it again.

PERSON #1: Hey, Fred, I noticed you punched in late this morning.

FRED: Hey, what's it to you? I'm the boss, you don't tell me what to do.

PERSON #1: I was just trying to see if everything's okay with you.

FRED: Hey, I didn't mean to snap. It's just Thursdays I go to couples' counseling.

PERSON #1: Oh, I guess I shouldn't have . . . I didn't mean to . . .

FRED: Oh, that's alright. You know we just adopted that baby, and I'm really jealous of the attention my wife gives it.

By making a vulnerable admission, Fred reversed his angry response and took the scene into new territory. Not only has he freed himself from the anger rut, he's also opened the door for transformation.

A Few Solutions . . .

EXERCISE 1: EMOTIONAL RANTS

It's hard to teach someone how to show just anger. It's easier to help someone first get in touch with all emotions, such as sadness, joy, fear, and anger. This exercise is designed to do that. It's a variation on a Keith Johnstone* exercise that's worked well in our workshops.

How It Works

Two people onstage: The Ranter, who needs to get emotional, and the other is The Helper.

The Helper offers a very bland, banal line, such as, "The pie is done," or "Your mom called." In reaction to this line, The Ranter begins a stream-of-consciousness rant that resembles a monologue. It needs to be a huge, over-the-top reaction, strong enough to sustain a two- or three-minute monologue. Let the emotion drive the words. If the emotion comes first, the words will naturally flow.

Then switch places, trading whose turn it is to be The Ranter.

Variation

Have four people do this exercise, and do the rants in pairs of two. This forces the players to mirror their partners' emotions. People's reactions grow stronger when they buddy-up and build off of each other.

Teaching Tips

If The Ranter appears to be stuck or inhibited, the teacher needs to assign emotions from the side after the banal line

---

*Keith Johnstone is the author of the classic text *Impro: Improvisation and the Theatre* (Mathuen).

is given. So take our example of "The pie is done." After that line is given, the teacher would then assign an emotion, such as giddy or sad. The Ranter rants, using the assigned emotion. It's a good idea to alternate the positive with the negative emotions.

If the class or group is inhibited overall, have them buddy-up and do repeated versions of the variation of this exercise.

Frequently improvisers are blocked completely. This is what's known as being "in your head." There is no worse state for improvisers—it's like having writers block onstage. The players are so focused on saying just the right thing, they cannot say anything at all. They are paralyzed. What we have found helpful for getting improvisers out of their heads is to get them into their bodies. The trick is to get them moving, to get them to physicalize the assigned emotion. If they are given *sadness*, side coach them to get on the floor in a ball. If they are assigned *scared*, have them cower in the corner. If they are assigned *excited*, encourage them to jump around. Sometimes it is as simple as reminding them to move, and then they connect to the emotion.

EXERCISE 2: AGREE THROUGH THE CONFLICT

This exercise gets players to understand that they can agree their way through conflict instead of arguing. Argument is blaming, and that usually doesn't get us anywhere.

How It Works

In this exercise two players are given a loaded scenario, ripe for disagreement. The one that we usually start off with is a cop pulling over a driver for committing a traffic violation. The focus is simple: have them agree their way through it and give specifics to support their agreement.

> COP: Do you know what you where doing?
> DRIVER: Yes, officer, I was doing 110 mph in 35 zone.
> COP: That's dangerous. You could have killed someone.

> DRIVER: I know. I was trying to kill myself. I just pro-
> posed to my girlfriend and she said no, because
> she never loved me.
> COP: Sounds like you have no reason to live.
> DRIVER: I don't, officer. That's why I drank a whole
> gallon of Tequila.
> COP: You're drunk. That is against the law. Get out
> of the car. (Driver gets out)
> DRIVER: I hope I get the death penalty.
> COP: I'll make sure of that.

That's the idea. Other scenarios we've used: boss firing employee, two people showing up for the same date, a couple in which someone had an affair, parents catching their teenagers having sex in their bed.

Teaching Tips

The tendency is for the players to argue since the deck seems stacked against agreement. But it's not really. Your job is to coach them to say *yes* to their partners' ideas even if it doesn't seem logical. A *yes* is *yes* in this exercise and we will take it any way we can get it. Our suggestion is if they don't say *yes*, stop them gently and remind them to say *yes* along with a specific piece of information. This will keep the scene moving forward. In the example scene we gave, the driver says *yes*, then adds specific information, such as "I was doing 110 mph in a 35 zone," and "that's why I drank a whole gallon of tequila." Those details are a lot more useful to the scene than saying, "I was going fast," or, "I was drinking." Specific information gives a scene its momentum. Be sure to enforce this, especially at the top of the scene.

Afraid of Naming People, Places, and Events

5

God is in the details.
—MIES VAN DER ROHE

Sometimes we see a scene in our workshop that's full of agreement. It should be a great scene, yet it isn't. It should be going forward, but it doesn't. We're left feeling empty, even though we heard a lot of *yeses*. Then it hits us: Nobody backed up their *yeses* with any specifics.

Scenes without specifics meander because nobody wants to make a mistake or make a move his partner may not understand. *Get off the improv fence and make a commitment to yourself and your scene partner.* You have to do more than just say *yes*. You have to ask yourself, "Why did my character do that?" and be specific with your responses.

Here's a quick example of a simple father/daughter scene:

DAUGHTER: You hit me.
FATHER: I am sorry.

No specifics, really no scene, just meandering. Here's that same scene with a specific or two:

DAUGHTER: You hit me, you bastard.

FATHER: Yeah, and I'll do again if I catch you sleeping around with that Parker boy.

Now we have some specifics and now we have the start of a scene. So if you want to make your job easier, always be specific. If you want to give more gifts, always be specific. After all, wouldn't it be fun in a later scene to play the Parker boy?

A Few Solutions . . .

EXERCISE 1: YES, BECAUSE CIRCLE

This is a justification exercise, because justifications usually involve details, and details can't help but nail down the people, places, and events.

How It Works

Have one person stand in the middle of a circle of people. The middle person will be doing the justifying. Let's call this person Amy. Amy will then turn to each person in the circle, and receive a line of dialogue. The lines can be as bland and straightforward as, "The bank is crowded today," or "I know I'm your teacher and it's probably wrong, but I'm in love with you."

Then after each line, it's Amy's job to respond with "Yes, because . . ." and then justify the statements back to the giver. Amy might say, "Yes, because it's a three-day weekend," or "Yes, you are in love with me, because I've been seducing you all semester, Mr. Gibson."

Teaching Tips

We really like this exercise because it forces the improviser to think about the *why* in a scene. *Why* is the bank crowded? *Why* is the teacher attracted to Amy? When you announce *why*, you must make big leaps of assumption, which is great. Improv is all about assumption, and people forget that.

So, the more specifics the better when answering *yes, because*. Be personal and specific with the justifications—that's how to create a rich scene.

EXERCISE 2: THREE-LINE SCENES

This is a classic way to determine the who, what, and where of a scene.

How It Works

Two people do a scene that has three lines total, performed one line at a time. An example might be,

PERSON #1: Hi, Marcie, I'm really excited to be here tonight.

PERSON #2: Me, too, Fred. We can finally sit in the Senior section of the bleachers.

PERSON #1: Guess what, my dad gave me a condom for after the game.

It may not be the most elegant scene in the world, but it gets the job done. We know those two people are seniors together, that they are at some game, sitting in the senior section of the bleachers, and that they might have sex tonight. That's what naming people, places, and things does—it gets the job done, and gives us a place to go.

Teaching Tips

Encourage the group to play this fast and furiously, and always include characters' names. That's really important!

Warning Label

The scenes might feel forced or a little mechanical, but that's okay. It shows what little effort is needed to ground a scene so that it may thrive.

Misguided Object Work 6

React to your object work like it's
the third person in the scene.
—JIMMY CARRANE

*E*verybody appreciates good object work. The
audience. The players. We feel it is both a vital
part of this art form and a great way to honor
it. We believe object work is important, but it
should support the scene, not distract from it.

We have all been taught to find something to do at
the top of the scene. Reach out into space and find an
object or an activity or grab something in the environment. But you should never ever do that at the
expense of your scene partner. We have seen this over
and over again in our workshops, an improviser making the object more important than the person she is
onstage with. *The primary connection is with the other
person and not the object; if you're not connecting with
your partner, your object work will be misguided.*

In classes at iOChicago, Del Close* used to yell at

---

*Del Close was the legendary guru of long-form improv, inven-
tor of the Harold, and cofounder of the iOChicago Theater with
Charna Halpern. This one sentence doesn't come close to
describing Del or his fantastic life. He was a huge influence on
us. After you've finished our book, go learn more about him.

people if they started a scene by digging a ditch or by any other physical activity. At the time, we could never figure out why. Now it's clear. The connection was misguided.

We are not saying that object work should be eliminated, but if it's interfering with that primary connection in the scene, it should be put on the back burner until the performer can walk and chew gum at the same time.

A Few Solutions . . .

EXERCISE 1: TWO-IN-ONE

We've been talking about putting object work aside, but we understand that's not always feasible. Here's an exercise about committing to object work, and then making it fit with your partner's choices.

How It Works

Two people start a scene, and at the top of that scene, each person must begin an activity before looking each other in the eye. Then the scene begins and they can look at one another, but without referencing the activity whatsoever! Over time, they will discover within the scene how these two very different activities exist together.

Here's an example Liz had in a class:

One person started by miming a shower, and the other person began on the ground, obviously working underneath a car. They were two feet apart. They never said, "Here we are in the car shop with a shower." Instead, as the scene unfolded, they discovered that they were married, and the wife had agreed to convert the master bedroom into an extra garage because she loved her husband. It was a tender and believable scene. They focused on one another and the relationship, slowly discovering where they were and who they were to each other.

Teaching Tips

This is incredibly important—they are not allowed to talk

about what they are doing at the top of the scene. Just keep doing it!

Don't let players bail by saying, "I see you've installed a shower in the garage." That would interrupt the discovery process. Trust and wait, trust and wait, trust and wait.

Warning Label

The scenes can get talky—just stay calm and stick to your guns.

EXERCISE 2: REALITY TRANSACTION SCENE

This demonstrates the beauty of being slow and real with your object work.

How it Works

Two people, offstage, pick a simple transaction on which to base a scene, such as going to a bank to cash a check, renting a video, or getting a cavity filled. The players decide who is the customer, and who is the worker. They will play these as simple straightforward people without attitude or strong personalities. Once it's cast and the environment determined, they will act out a simple transaction.

For instance, in a real bank when someone is cashing a check, the teller might ask for picture ID, check the computer, ask for the customer's mother's maiden name for security purposes, ask how the customer wants the money, and so forth. These are the details the players need to show the reality of this transaction.

The more specific the players can be in this exercise, the more vivid it will be for them and the audience. If you create a video store, is it a chain store or is it the neighborhood independent store? Those two stores and their selections and procedures are different. These differences should appear in the exercise.

Teaching Tips

Stress that this exercise is not a scene. We want to see what really happens when someone goes into a store to make a purchase. Imagine we are almost eavesdropping on this. The players need not to be rushed; we have seen this scene go for five or six minutes.

Some tips to avoid misguided object work:

- First of all, stop talking about what you're doing. Just do it. Don't name it; it may be named for you, or you may have to adjust it according to what the scene needs.
- The simpler the better!
- Latch onto someone else's object work. Start doing what he is doing, especially if you don't have a clue what he is doing! That's when the real fun begins.
- Start with a strong action, but make eye contact with your partners, and invite them emotionally into your improvising.
- If all else fails, drop your object work and go to the connection.

You Are Required to Play the Opposite Sex | 7

Bite off more than you can chew,
then chew it.
—ELLA WILLIAMS

We've seen this situation in the workshop a million times. Someone names another player to be an opposite-sex character, and that player freezes up like a deer caught in headlights. Afterward, we ask the frozen player, why didn't you play the opposite sex? And we usually hear back, "I didn't know I could," or "I didn't know I was supposed to."

Well, we're telling you, you should. It's a gift. Your fellow player is giving you a gift. So just take the gift.

We've seen where it's *obvious* a character that could be the opposite sex is being called for in a scene, and no one steps out. For example, there's a scene with a father and son, and they're calling for a mother, but nobody enters the scene! Everyone on the back line is looking at each other, waiting for a woman to enter. We're saying *anyone* should enter—man, woman, or beast. Afterward we ask the statues from the back line, why didn't one of you step out? Again we hear, "I didn't know I could," or "I didn't know I was supposed to."

Well, you can. So do it, and get over it. Not only

is it okay to play the opposite sex, it's required. We're moving on to the next chapter.

A Few Solutions . . .

How It Works

If you're a male, the next time you improvise, play a female. If you're a female . . . um, let's see . . . play a male.

Teaching Tips

It's especially important to practice playing opposite genders in rehearsals, because some people need to get used to the idea.

Warning Label

Make these choices from the top of your intelligence. Avoid stereotypes! Not all guys grab their crotches; not all girls speak in high, ditzy voices. The more realistically you can portray the opposite sex, the more rewarding it will be for you, your teammates, and the audience.

Fear of Playing Politically Incorrect Characters

8

I think you need to relax your crack.
—SUSAN MESSING

We have seen this situation also over and over in our workshops, players afraid to go the Dark Side or portray a politically incorrect character, because they're afraid when they come offstage people will think the offensive character is who they really are. They have stopped themselves before they've even started. This limits their choices and stifles their imagination. At that point, we are not seeing life onstage, but a sanitized version. Why go out to see improv? You might as well stay home and watch TV.

One of your jobs onstage is to portray life, real life, life that is uncomfortable and sometimes politically incorrect, or even impolite. Remember, an improviser is an actor. The only difference is that you are writing the dialogue as you go. You will be asked, if you are lucky, to play racists, murderers, and pirates. When Carroll O'Connor played Archie Bunker, did people think he was really a bigot? Or Anthony Hopkins really a serial killer? Or Johnny Depp a pirate?

31

A Few Solutions . . .

EXERCISE 1: TABOO TOPIC MONOLOGUES

Taboo topics are subject matter that makes you jumpy—child abuse, racism, sexual abuse, alcoholism, rape. You get the idea.

The intention of this exercise is to break open the way you play, to remove the reservations inside your mind that say "I can't say *that*," "I can't do a scene about *that*," "I can't do *that*."

How It Works

Each class member writes down a taboo topic on a slip of paper that goes into a hat. Pulling a slip from the hat, one person does a monologue directly related to that slip's topic. (It's up to the teacher to decide if the topic should be announced before or after the monologue.) So, if the suggestion is pet torturer, the character must have committed pet torture, or witnessed it, or been involved closely. This should just be a short character monologue.

Note: Look out for unexpected laughs. If the topic pulled is child pornography, not much will be creepier or funnier than a starting sentence such as, "She had long blonde hair, it glistened. It was shinier than any of the other third graders on the playground that day."

Teaching Tips

Encourage everyone who does a monologue to dive into the deep dark depths of the taboo topic! This won't work if played with reservation.

These are character monologues. The improvisers need not have witnessed pet torture (thank goodness), but must be willing to make up a character from their dark side.

Be prepared, because this exercise might make you or your fellow improvisers uncomfortable. Which is good, we think.

Warning Label Number 1

People are gonna balk. They'll pretend like they don't know how to do this, or can't, or it's too intimidating. Don't buy it. We've found that every improviser has a twisted dark side clamoring to get out.

Warning Label Number 2

Everyone will probably be very worried about offending the audience. Fuck 'em. The audience can take care of itself. As an improviser, you must not avoid touchy topics.

EXERCISE 2: TABOO TOPIC SCENES

How It Works

Use the same hat of taboo topics from Exercise 1. Have two people do a scene based on one of these topics. The scene must be *directly* related to the subject on the paper. If the suggestion was incest, then yes, we must see a scene about incest. Not necessarily the incest event itself, but its aftermath—a scene about those affected.

Here's an example:

SISTER: Didn't expect to see you at Aunt Shirley's funeral. Don't hug me in front of Mom anymore. It's like she reads us.

BROTHER: It only happened a couple dozen times. What are you so uptight about?

SISTER: I think Mom knows, and she thinks it's my fault.

BROTHER: It was. You were a cheerleader.

SISTER: You're an asshole.

BROTHER: You've gained weight. Don't worry, I wouldn't sleep with you now.

Don't dance around the topic! Be sure to play the scenes real and hard, or else they will ring hollow.

Teaching Tips

These topics are going to make people uncomfortable. It's the teacher's job to give the class permission to go "there," wherever "there" might be.

Warning Label

We are not saying: go out and intentionally do a scene that is graphic or offensive just for the sake of being graphic or offensive. What we are saying is that if a taboo topic is appropriate and it's what everyone is feeling, don't back away from it. If the scene is calling for it, then you can, and you must, go "there."

By the Way, It's Acting | 9

Acting is all about honesty. If you can
fake that, you've got it made.
—George Burns

*I*mprovisers don't want to act in their scenes any-more. Instead, they want to talk their way through them. Acting your way through a scene is becoming all but obsolete, and that troubles us. Being clever has become a substitute for acting. Improvisers are trying incredibly hard to be witty, as if that is the only skill they need. Unfortunately this gets rewarded with laughter, and even worse, the improviser develops a bad habit.

We feel it's important to remind everyone that you have a choice: you can strive to create something that is more like theater, that may move people emotion-ally, or you can strive to create something that is more like bad stand-up, that hopefully people will forget. You may think that reaching for emotional depth in improv is unrealistic. In some respects it is. And we would be the first to tell you, we don't always live up to it, but it is what we strive for most of the time.

The strongest moments of improv come when you let go and follow your instinct and don't think, just react. This is acting your way through a scene. And it seems to come when you let your emotions take over, allowing your character to feel strongly about an issue or circumstance.

For example, it's exciting to watch a character get terrific news, like winning the Publishers Clearing House lottery. Then he starts crying because change is really scary and his family's going to be calling all the time for money. Then he gets excited because finally his dad is going to take an interest in him. Then he remembers his dad never had time for him growing up, he becomes angry and rips up the check. Now the delivery guy, who's a nineteen-year-old slacker taking two classes at the junior college, starts crying because he's afraid he's going to get fired and his dad is going to kick him out of the basement.

Your job as an actor is to take someone's words and bring them to life with real emotion. Make them your own. Your job as improviser is to take your words and bring them to life with real emotions. Make them believable. Great actors don't necessarily make great improvisers, and vice versa, but having acting skills and emotional commitment helps bring authenticity to your work. No matter how funny or clever you are, remember, it's ultimately acting.

A Few Solutions . . .

EXERCISE 1: STANDING IN LINE AT THE BURGER KING®

The benefit of this exercise is that if subtext can be useful in such a simple transaction scene as this, imagine how powerful subtext can be in a more intimate scene.

How It Works

Three or four improvisers stand in line at Burger King®. One improviser is the employee, a bland, neutral character.

One at a time, each character comes up to the counter and places an order. How and what each character orders tells much about what type of person each character is.

For example, Phil, a martyr who's decided subconsciously he'll never get a break in life, goes up to the counter.

PHIL: Geez . . . you guys raised your prices.
BK: Yeah, the Whopper® is thirty-two cents more.
Phil: Great. I don't have enough now. I haven't eaten all day. Just gimme a soda, I'll skip the rest. I hope I have enough for that. Can I get a straw, or is that extra?

So while you're in line, quickly make a decision about your character, and then speak from that decision. Ask yourself, "What's my character's biggest want or fear in life?" It should be something psychological, like, "Wants to get laid, but will never act on it," or "Afraid of rejection." This will become your character's subtext, the driving force that's never discussed, but motivates every choice a character makes. You will learn to act from the subtext, not talk about it.

Have each improviser go through this exercise several times.

Variation

Each character can turn to the class and announce what his or her deep want or fear is, and then turn back and place the order. That's fun, because you get to see inside the character's head before he speaks.

Teaching Tips

Encourage people to find their characters' traits by standing or moving differently as they are waiting in line at the Burger King®. The body can provide information about a character before the improviser even knows it. Remind students that if they are slumping over, or hesitant to speak, or nervously tapping a foot, that's a basis for great subtext.

EXERCISE 2: COMA

This is an acting exercise designed to highlight what's really going on in a relationship.

How It Works

Round One ■ Get onstage two at a time. One of the people will render his character unable to speak at the top of the scene. For example, listening to music with headphones, or being in deep meditation or prayer, or passed out, or even dead. It must be a believable, real reason why the character can't speak. Then it is the job of the other person to carry the whole scene verbally. Much like emotional rants, it's a stream-of-consciousness monologue, and by the end the player will have established who the two are to each other, how they feel, and where they are.

Here's an example:

> One improviser lays down onstage. The second improviser, a man, enters a room to find a young woman lying on the floor. He checks her pulse to discover she's still alive, and he's relieved. He discovers an empty prescription bottle on the floor. He looks at her with contempt and despair. "You fucking bitch," he whispers, "you were gonna make it. I'm done saving you. You can save yourself this time. I vowed never to love a patient, but I couldn't help himself with you. And to overdose in my office? Great." Then he becomes sad. He's devastated by her actions and bends over her body crying. "You stupid, stupid woman," he murmurs, "tonight was going to be. . . . I've been waiting my whole life to find you." He pulls out an engagement ring. "You don't deserve this, you bitch."

Round Two ■ Now flip the talking part in each pair. The person who spoke in Round One is now in a coma and unable to speak during the entire scene of Round Two. This coma scene can take place in time before or after Round One.

To continue the example from above,

> The overdosing woman is now sitting in a chair next to the man, who's in a coma. She holds his hand

against her face, sadly. "I know I should have married you," she says, "I'm clean now. I've changed, Terrence. I was an idiot. You saved me so many times. You should have let me die. Don't die. Please pull through this. I'll get a divorce and we'll be together. I promise, this time will be better. I've gotta go, Terrence. I love you." And she pulls a bottle of Vicadin from her purse and takes three pills, sipping from his glass of water.

Teaching Tip

Have the pairs go through Round One without telling them about the coma that lies ahead in Round Two. Prepare everyone by explaining that these scenes are thoughtful and real, not wacky and hilarious. This is an exercise to get the acting muscle going—make them act!

We've noticed our students feel very fulfilled after this exercise. Encourage them to be dramatic because that's where they want to go.

It's Not the Words, It's the Connection

10

Slow motion will get you there faster.
—HOAGY CARMICHAEL

*L*ook, there is an unspoken current that runs between you and your scene partner. It comes before you even open your mouth and comes directly off your partner. This is where the vein of gold lies. So when we say, *It's not the words, it's the connection*, we mean the nonverbal connection. The nonverbal connection is the silence between you and your partner before you think the scene has begun. It's your gut feeling about that person in that first moment. Is he your brother? The boyfriend who dumped you? The girl you know you'll marry? The scene may not play out like this, but you've got to start somewhere. Let yourself feel that nonverbal connection.

It's as though improvisers don't even know the connection is there. Instead, people just talk too much. They think the words will sustain them. How wrong they are. Words can be an avoidance of what is really going on in the relationship, and the relationship is everything underneath the words.

We see it in our workshops and classes, people searching so hard in their heads to find the scene . . .

like the scene is even in their heads. They are focusing all their energies inwardly and thinking about what they should say, when they need to be focused outwardly, on their partner. If they would just slow down, even for a second or two, and interpret the silence, they would actually find the scene more quickly.

Learning to connect nonverbally is a developed muscle. Words come from your head. The connection comes from your being. It's about connecting with your partner on an emotional level first, and then letting the dialogue come second. Unfortunately, most improvisers have this reversed.

Improvising is about collaboration; it's an art form that you can't do alone. If you're up there just talking and not connecting, you're not improvising, you're masturbating.

A Few Solutions . . .

EXERCISE 1: GETTING CONNECTED

This isn't so much a scenic exercise, as it is a way to get players to read what's going on underneath a scene. It works the connection muscle.

How It Works

Have the players walk around onstage making eye contact with their partners. As they walk around have them notice what is going on with their partners emotionally. Are they tired or hung over? Are they excited or sad? Are they angry or happy? We tell students all the time to "focus on your partner," yet we need to let them know what to focus on. For us, the focus should be the emotional state their partner is in.

When you feel the players have got the energy flowing, pair them off, facing each other about three feet apart. (If you do not have an even number of players, have someone sit out and then rotate back in.)

Round One ■ Have them look at their partners, taking in their whole body, eyes, language, emotions. Then ask each player from each group what they are getting off each other emotionally. "He seems angry," or "She seems sad." This is good emotional data.

Ask each group the same question.

Round Two ■ Go back to the first group and ask one person to define the relationship: are they brothers, boyfriend/girlfriend, coworkers, mother/daughter, and so on.

Round Three ■ Ask the other player what is going on between the two characters. The answers must be specific, as in, "She is my younger sister and she's screwed up. She is on drugs and if our parents find out they will kick her out of the house." Or, "He is my Dad and I know he is having an affair with my aunt." The more specific the better. Reinforce that scenes need to have stakes, life-and-death stakes.

Teaching Tips

Round Three is the most crucial round because most improvisers will want to be vague. Don't let them. They will they say, "I did something wrong," or "She has some good news for me." We want them to be more specific and make the stakes high, so high we get a bloody nose from watching. This is a scene and not a conversation. Side coach the players to name what specifically their character did wrong or what specifically the good news is about; otherwise, this exercise becomes stuck in vague-land.

EXERCISE 2: NUMBERS ONE THROUGH FIFTY

This is a great exercise to reinforce the concept that it's not the *words,* but the *tension* that can drive a scene. (We'd like to thank Michael Gellman* for introducing this exercise to Jimmy.)

---

*Michael J. Gellman is a senior faculty member of the Second City Training Center in Chicago and program head at the Second City Training Center in New York. He is the coauthor with Mary Scruggs of *Process: An Improviser's Journey.*

How It Works

Let the players know that they will only get to speak in this exercise by literally saying numbers as their dialogue until they get to the number fifty. Such as,

PLAYER A: One, Two.
PLAYER B: Three.
PLAYER A: Four, Five, Six.
PLAYER B: Seven.

The players can say as many numbers as they want at a time, but we stress that, as in any improv scene, each player says a line and waits for response. Remember, even in an exercise like this, it's about give-and-take. Stimulus and response.

Prior to starting, give them a premise to begin in silence. It should be a premise filled with tension, such as: Underage girl hooks up with her older brother's best friend for a one-night stand. The scene starts the next morning and they are waking up silent on his futon. Or, two same-sex coworkers have worked in the same office for years. Last night at the office party one person kissed the other. The scene begins the next morning in the cubicle at work, silent. Or an absentee/abusive father left the family when the grown child were very young. The adult child has not heard from the father for fifteen years, and he shows up, needing two hundred dollars. The scene starts silent with dad in the child's apartment.

When the teacher/director feels the players are connected, they are given permission to use the crutch dialogue of the numbers. The focus in this exercise is connecting to the tension and the scene partner. If they do that, they won't want have to work to find the scene; it will actually find them.

Teaching Tips

Be flexible. Most players don't start really connecting until they are into the high teens or low twenties, so if they are connecting, don't feel you have to cut them off at fifty. Be flexible and let them go past the number fifty. The important thing is for them to experience the connection.

Another good tip to help them connect even deeper is to assign something for one or both the characters. For example, in the legendary hook-up scene, you can say beforehand that the boyfriend is in love with the girl, or that he didn't tell her he has an STD, or he was a virgin. You can add that the girl in the scene already has a boyfriend, or that she is not interested in him except for sex, or that she was just using him to get back at her brother.

Warning Label

Everybody rushes through this exercise. Slow down for success.

Lack of Trust | *11*

To be trusted is a greater
compliment than to be loved.
—George McDonald

T hroughout these workshops, we've seen
improvisers either not trusting each other
or not trusting themselves onstage. Learning to trust either of these things is about
learning to have faith in the unknown, and it is one of
the hardest lessons for any improviser. We think your
ultimate goal as an improviser should be to *let go*,
which means going somewhere you had no intention of going. This is only accomplished by surrender-
ing to the group.

See, lack of trust is wanting to control. It's a reaction to not knowing what is going to happen next
onstage. It's the opposite of improvisation. When you
are trying to control, you are no longer making discoveries along with the group; you are working exclu-
sively with your fear, which, by the way, has terrible
ideas. By not putting your trust in the group, there is
no way you can let go, and if you can't let go, you
aren't really improvising. You're faking it.

The improv holy grail, that experience we are
constantly seeking as performers, is that rare time
when it feels like someone is putting the words in our

mouths. We are no longer working, something is working us. When it comes, we don't know. How often it comes, we can't tell you. What we can tell you is you ain't going to get there by yourself. You need the group to take you there. Isn't that why you chose this art form in the first place, to work with others?

A Few Solutions . . .

EXERCISE 1: AWKWARD AFTERMATH

This exercise demonstrates the power of trust between two people to interrupt the silence in a scene.

How It Works

Two people sit in chairs at a table in a restaurant, in silence. They must interpret the silence because someone has just shared big news. It can be good news, like a promotion at work, or devastating news, like having just learned of a miscarriage. Whatever the news was, it was meaningful.

So, first they sit in silence, feeling out what type of information was shared, and by whom. Though they are in silence, the scene has begun and they are being affected by one another and the tension of the silence. They sit for at least a minute in silence before they speak.

In order to discover the news, they must find it together line by line. For example,

LINE EXERCISE 1: It's okay. We'll find another house.
LINE EXERCISE 2: I thought you'd be really upset.
LINE EXERCISE 3: I am. You're careless. (Pause.) Thanks for admitting what you did.
LINE EXERCISE 4: I really didn't think a toaster could start a house fire.
LINE EXERCISE 5: Yeah. Well, now we know.

They sit for a while in silence again, soaking up the awkward aftermath of their discoveries, speaking when they feel the need to. This scene can be short, about two minutes, or go for five minutes or more.

EXERCISE 2: GETTING CONNECTED (FROM CHAPTER 11)

This isn't so much a scenic exercise, as it is a way to get players to read what's going on underneath a scene. It works the connection muscle.

How It Works

Have the players walk around onstage making eye contact with their partners. As they walk around have them notice what is going on with their partners emotionally. Are they tired or hung over? Are they excited or sad? Are they angry or happy? We tell students all the time to "focus on your partner," yet we need to let them know what to focus on. For us, the focus should be the emotional state their partner is in.

When you feel the players have got the energy flowing, pair them off, facing each other about three feet apart. (If you do not have an even number of players, have someone sit out and then rotate back in.)

Round One ■ Have them look at their partners, taking in their whole body, eyes, language, emotions. Then ask each player from each group what they are getting off each other emotionally. "He seems angry," or "She seems sad." This is good emotional data.

Ask each group the same question.

Round Two ■ Go back to the first group and ask one person to define the relationship: are they brothers, boyfriend/girlfriend, coworkers, mother/daughter, and so on.

Round Three ■ Ask the other player what is going on between the two characters. The answers must be specific, as in, "She is my younger sister and she's screwed up. She is on drugs and if our parents find out they will kick her out of the house." Or, "He is my Dad and I know he is having an affair with my aunt." The more specific the better. Reinforce that scenes need to have stakes, life-and-death stakes.

Now when we look back over this scene, it becomes apparent what the big news was. It's as if someone said at the beginning, "Look, Helen—I'm the one who burned the house down." We never actually heard that line, but it affected the whole scene.

Teaching Tips

Watch that the improvisers don't just blurt out the news. The improvisers do not actually say what the news was at the beginning, nor do they assign who has the news. They interpret all this from the silence once the scene begins.

The words must match the silence. If a status game was implied in the silence, enforce it when they are speaking. Don't let the improvisers panic and go to easy choices. If the tension was high in the silence, so should the tension be with words.

Warning Label

Most improvisers think that it has to be a heavy, dreary scene. It does not. We've seen this be a very positive exercise that allows improvisers to read each other in the silence, and see that the scene is written there long before words are used.

Choosing the Funny over the Craft

12

> It took me four years to stop sucking.
> —MILES STROTH

W hen we first started out improvising, we wanted to prove we were funny. Going for the laugh seemed like the right thing to do. But the longer we hung around and the longer we improvised, the more we realized this was a craft and going for the joke was stunting our growth. We may have been the funniest people from college or at parties, but that didn't necessarily translate to the stage. We needed to be taught.

Improvisation is a skill. *The choice is simple: either you can learn the craft that will ultimately make you even funnier, or you can rely solely on your wit and take your chances.* Being a good improviser and being funny are not synonymous.

After some years, we finally got it through our thick heads that the goal was not to go out and intentionally be funny as much as it was to build. Build relationships. Build solid scene work. Build a whole piece of theater with our partners. We learned to trust. Trust that we did not have to work so hard. Trust that the funny would come to us. Trust that we would see it, and smell it, and feel it. It was different kind of funny. It was filling and nutritious.

In our workshops, we see many students who focus on just being funny and ignore the craft. These people justify in their heads that if they are getting the laughs they must be doing it right. But they are doing it at the expense of good scene work. These improvisers usually aren't as funny as they think.

Becoming a craftsman takes faith. It takes patience. It takes time. Del Close made us believe that. We hope someday we are lucky enough to make you believe that, so you can learn from our mistakes.

A Solution . . .

INTENTIONALLY DON'T GET A LAUGH

You heard us right. The idea here is to see how grounded, real, serious, and *unfunny* the beginning of a piece can be.

How It Works

Make an agreement with your fellow players that you all will work very hard *not* to get a laugh in the first couple of scenes of your next performance. Your group could come up with the specifics, like limit not getting a laugh to the first six minutes. What will happen is that by not being funny in the beginning, you'll build for bigger and better laughs later in the piece. Trust us. If you do this assignment, it will happen. If you build serious scenes, the laughs will come.

Warning Label

If you are pregnant or nursing a baby, have high blood pressure or hypertension, you may experience dizziness. Seek advice from a health care professional before using this exercise.

The Improv Committee Resides in Your Head

Those whose approval you seek most,
give you the least.
—MAURICE CHEVALIER

"The Improv Committee resides in your head" is a phrase we use in our workshops for a performer who seems to be playing for the approval of the so-called respected people in the community. These "Improv Committee" members can come in many forms. They may be the elder statesmen who sit at the end of the bar in your theater, watching, stone-faced, apparently passing judgment on the performance. They could be an artistic director, a teacher, a producer, or perhaps another group of improvisers or peers.

When we see an improviser who is playing for the committee's approval, we see someone who is confused and conflicted. Mostly that improviser is lost, like a child searching for missing parents. He is playing to impress the committee, yet he doesn't know what the committee is looking for, so really, this improviser is only guessing. *It's hard enough to be in your own head, let alone someone else's.*

We see a similar expression on the faces of these improvisers seeking the committee's respect, one of constant waiting. Waiting for a response. Waiting to make the right move. Waiting for validation. This waiting makes it almost impossible to be spontaneous. As a result, these improvisers are never in the moment, but on a three-second delay.

The problem is simple: they are serving two masters at once, their scene partner and the committee, and in the process are serving neither. They are forced to pick sides between their own instincts and their need for outside validation and in the process they lose out.

We believe that in this art form, part of your job is to discover your own voice. Unfortunately, you will need to take chances, lots and lots of chances, for you to truly accomplish this. And realistically there is no wrong way to do this. What works for one does not work for another. This is where your journey begins. We said this before, but this time we mean it: There's only one way to improvise: yours.

A Solution . . .

The thing to remember is that although the improv committee people may be real, your need for their approval is not. That is in your head.

Approval is not something you can attain by striving for it. When you think you've achieved it, it will disappear, and it will never be enough. And this will drive you crazy.

Approval is like getting hooked on crack; it is death to your craft. Seeking outside validation on stage is self-indulgent. It is selfish: you're not serving your partner, you are serving your own needs. In order to get out of yourself, you must focus on others.

Chasing the committee from your head is about making a personal choice more than it is about doing an improv exercise. It involves making a shift in your thinking. We are not saying this is easy. We have both struggled with these approval issues, and at times we still do. You need to go from "How I am being perceived?" to "What is needed by my partner?" Just like in your life, when you take time out to listen to a friend's problems, you forget about yourself for that ten minutes, because you are of service to someone else. That's the shift: to forget about you and start giving.

Teaching Tips

We get this question all the time: "How do I teach a person who's playing for others' approval?" The answer is to love them. Love them. You gotta give them all the love and support you can muster. Until they drive you nuts; then kick them out of the group.

Warning Label

Be patient, and realize that a lot more than approval as an improviser is at stake.

Stop Wanting | *14*

Improv is a tricky mistress—the more you want from her, the less you'll get.
—LIZ ALLEN

S top wanting the audience to like you. Stop wanting to get your emotional needs met. Stop wanting to get laid. Stop wanting everyone to love you. Stop wanting the approval of others. Stop wanting to look cool. Stop wanting to look smart. Stop wanting to be politically correct. Stop wanting to be popular. Stop wanting to be someone else. Stop wanting to make up for your childhood. Stop wanting to be funny. Stop wanting to get people to do what you want. Stop wanting a development deal. Stop wanting to be class president. Stop wanting to be discovered. Stop wanting to be a rock star.

We have seen all sorts of people have all sorts of unrealistic expectations from improv. And we have seen those people go crazy, get in their own way and not live up to their full potential. They are dying a sad improv death; unfortunately they just don't know it.

We aren't saying don't dream. We love that. If you want more out of your career than improv, then you need to do more than just improvise. What we are saying is, don't put unrealistic expectations on this art form. It's as simple as that. The only expectation you need is to improve every time you perform. You may not be getting approval from the audience, you may not be getting a development deal, and you may not be getting laid. What you are doing is honing your craft and becoming a better improviser.

A Solution . . .

Stop wanting.

Yes *Begins Offstage*

15

The artist is nothing without the gift,
but the gift is nothing without work.
—EMILE ZOLA

Agreement is an attitude. It's something that is not limited to just the stage. It begins when you walk through the door. Too often improvisers bring in the wrong attitude. Bitterness. Entitlement. Arrogance. These do nothing but interfere with their stage work. It is no coincidence that the people who struggle with saying *yes* on stage are the most defiant off.

In one of our early workshops, an improviser showed up late. He came in with an arrogant, I've-paid-for-this-workshop-so-I-can-show-up-whenever-I-want attitude. Our guess, he was maybe still drunk, and he was completely unapologetic. In just a matter of minutes, our first impression was, this guy's trouble. What did his behavior say to the group? It said: Fuck you.

Whether he knew it or not, he had already broken the rules. With being late. With being drunk. With his attitude. When we follow the rules in improv, both onstage and off, we build trust, create ensemble, and protect the group. Being on time, being cooperative and showing up in working condition are no different

59

from saying *yes*. These are rules, and we have all agreed to play by them, and if we don't, we don't have ensemble.

Most improvisers don't want to be accountable. They don't want to make a commitment, and they are always looking for the exception to the rule. And if you don't play by the rules, you run the risk of getting a reputation for being hard to work with. You don't want to be hard to work with. Improv is a small community, and a very tiny list, and we know everyone on it. Reputations follow people like the dust cloud around Pigpen from the *Peanuts* comic strip.

We have seen mediocre improvisers rise to the top because they understood hard work and accountability, which should inspire us all. On the flip side, we have seen phenomenal improvisers never reach their potential because they didn't get it, which should scare the shit out of all of us.

We by no means are saying to be a doormat and roll over and play dead. That is not productive to you or to the group. We encourage you always to speak your truth and make your point. Remember, improv is acting, and some of our best acting happens offstage.

A Few Solutions . . .

EXERCISE 1: DON'T GET ON THE LIST

Watch your attitude. We have seen a ton of performers bring a ton of baggage to the rehearsal process, and infect the entire group with their bad attitudes. It only takes one person. Most of the time it's done with very few words or no words at all. Sulking and brooding require little effort.

EXERCISE 2: GO OUTSIDE THE IMPROV COMMUNITY

Improv can be therapeutic but it's not therapy; it's an art form. So treat it like an art form. If you need emotional support, go outside the group to find it. We have a theory that most improvisers come from dysfunctional families, so it's not surprising that this can be a dysfunctional art from.

Find healthy people you can trust, who will listen and help you find a solution to your problems. Try getting into real therapy, or a support group or a twelve-step program.

EXERCISE 3: FUCKING SAY THANK YOU

When we started out performing we were terrible about receiving compliments. Someone would come up to us after a performance and say, "Great show," and we'd have some excuse like, "You should have been here last night," or, "We were a little off." Who wants to hear that *shit?* Instead we should have shut our pieholes after uttering two little words: *Thank You.*

Spreading Yourself Too Thin

16

If you want to do a million things,
you can do a million things,
but nobody said you'll be any good at them.
—GREBS

*I*f improv is supposed to be about life, and your life is filled with nothing more than improv, then your improv becomes about improv, and that's boring! You are probably burned out but don't realize it, and most likely overcommitted. You are improvising so much, and wondering why you aren't getting better. It's simple: you don't make time to have a life. Improv needs to be fed by enriching experiences that are unrelated to performance.

Take the time to read a book that isn't about improv (but this book doesn't count), get a good night's sleep, go to a concert—all these things enrich your life and at the same time enrich your improv. See the connection? If you're improvising way too much and are overcommitting to three or four projects at a time, the work becomes mired down and mediocre, and the implosion is evident.

We feel spreading yourself too thin has become an epidemic. We would even say, in some cases, that it's become an addiction. These improvisers become addicted to the stage time. They are stage addicts. You can see it in their eyes; they have nothing left.

Quantity replaces quality. We have seen plenty of improvisers start out with the potential to become true artists, but end up burnt-out stage junkies.

In Chicago, we've noticed improvisers are spreading themselves so thin that they don't make time to go and see improv shows. They are ripping themselves off of one of the most valuable tools for learning improv: watching improv. When we started out we went to the all the improv shows. If they were bad, we learned what not to do. If they were good, we were inspired. If your goal is to become a mediocre improviser, nothing will ensure your success quicker than to overcommit, not go see improv, and not have a life.

A Few Solutions . . .

When a new improv opportunity comes along and you feel your plate is full, here are three questions we think will help you make your decision about taking the opportunity or giving it up.

1. How many nights a week are you already involved in improv/acting/performing?

    Warning Sign: If it's two or more, you are in dangerous territory.

    Let's do the math here. Suppose you are doing two shows a week. How often do you rehearse? If the group is any good, we hope at least once a week for a good two- to three-hour chunk. So, two shows and two rehearsals, you are now busy about four nights a week. Plus, let's say you are taking a class on Saturdays; there goes another three hours, not counting travel time. What about watching some improv shows? Add another three hours. What's that, about 18 hours? When you get down to it, there is really not much time left to have a real life, and that is a prerequisite to doing this kind of work. If you don't have a life offstage, you ain't going to find one onstage.

If you feel burned out, the remedy won't be found in your work, but in your life. Is your life big enough or is it just filled with improv? If it's just improv, we suggest: Take a break. Regroup. Get a real life. The worse thing that can happen is you will come back to improv refreshed and with a sparkling new perspective.

2. Are you truly excited about the project, the people, the director?

Warning Sign: If you're only taking on this project so you won't miss out on the "next big thing," you are in dangerous territory.

3. If this project is so important, are you willing to drop or take a break from another commitment to do make room for this one?

Warning Sign: If you the answer is no, you may be a stage addict or maybe this project isn't for you. Either way, you are in dangerous territory.

Improv Is Bigger Than You Think 17

I have met the enemy and it is myself.

—POGO

We hear improvisers in Chicago say all the time, "I didn't get on a team" at the ioChicago, or "I didn't get hired by Second City." They become beaten down and bitter. Their careers are over at age twenty-two. They have blown their only chance. They act like there are only two places to improvise in a city that probably has hundreds of groups performing weekly. We wish this problem only occurred in Chicago, but we have experienced this in smaller cities as well.

During the last twenty years in Chicago, we've seen many great groups, shows, and theaters created because performers weren't getting their needs met at other venues. They stopped complaining and started creating. We were lucky enough to be a part of some of these groups, which provided not only creative high points in our careers, but also long-lasting contributions to the community.

In an art form that is about making it up as you go along, it appears for some improvisers that skill only applies to the stage. *Remember, improvisation is larger than all the institutions combined, and those places aren't stopping you from performing. You are.* Improvisers are funny, imaginative, and spontaneous onstage. But when it comes to actually finding the stage to perform on, they can be uncreative, rigid, and downright depressing. Those improvisers are trading away all their power for the permission to perform, waiting for a person, place, or thing to validate their desires. We can tell you this: it ain't a fair trade. You're ripping yourself off. If you keep looking for outside validation and emotional support you are going to get crushed on a daily basis.

The point is you have to decide if you want to do this. Not Jimmy. Not Liz. Not your parents. Not your director. Not your friends. *You*. So stop bitching and create.

A Few Solutions . . .

Start your own group. Be organized and be professional. Set your guidelines and hold people accountable. Improvisers are lazy. They are accustomed to just showing up, so the more you can plan and get things in place (a venue, a director, a rehearsal schedule), the more quality people you can attract to a project.

Teaching Tips

Direct your own group. Be organized and be professional. Set your guidelines and hold people accountable. Improvisers are lazy. They just want to show up. Make it clear from the start what you expect—scheduling, policy on missed rehearsals, call times, and most importantly the consequences. By setting these boundaries, the more quality people you can attract to your project.

Warning Label

Some people may balk, especially the overcommitted. Some people may drop out, especially the overcommitted. Some people you may have to ask to leave, especially the overcommitted. Commitment is kryptonite to the improviser. Your goal is to create an ensemble, not just another under-rehearsed and uninspired improv group; there are plenty of those out there.

Love the Process | 18

*L*ove the process. Love it. Because with improv you are always in it. Improvisation is pure process. So love it. Accept it. Because you'll never be doing exactly the same thing again, which is what makes it so fascinating. A long-form show takes anywhere from four to six times in front of an audience to figure itself out, if we are lucky. That is process. Pure process. And when we are not enjoying it, it sucks. We want to blame. We want to quit.

Recently this happened to Jimmy when he returned to performing. After a series of rough shows, he started to blame. The ensemble wasn't playing the way he thought they should. He wanted to quit. After six weeks he finally figured it out: He wasn't in process, he was in fear. Until he was willing to humble himself, he was miserable. So love the process.

Love the good shows, because they don't last forever.

Love the bad shows, because they don't last forever.

Love the rehearsals, because your best work will happen there.

Love your casts, because you'll learn from the bad ones as well as the good ones.

Love your directors, because you'll learn from the bad ones as well as the good ones.

Love your choices, because you'll learn from the bad ones as well as the good ones.

Biographies

Liz Allen

Liz received the Coach of the Year award at The Del Close Awards three years straight after teaching at the iOChicago. She was a member of iOChicago's Frank Booth, and coached Valhalla, Mission Improvable, and Fatty Four Eyes. She co-teaches the Individual Assessment Workshop with Jimmy. Liz recently moved to Las Vegas with her family and directed The Second City's revue at the Flamingo Hotel. Liz may be contacted at lizallenimprov@comcast.net.

Jimmy Carrane

Jimmy has taught at The Second City, The Annoyance, and Victory Gardens Theater in Chicago. He currently teaches The Art of Slow Comedy at the iOChicago, as well as co-teaching the Individual Assessment Workshop with Liz. He was an original member of The Annoyance Theater and the groundbreaking long-form supergroup Jazz Freddy. Jimmy lives in Chicago, where he is a commercial actor and is a regular contributor for Chicago public radio. Jimmy may be contacted at jcarrane@aol.com.

71